JUJU JAZZ
P O E T I C S

J. PLUNKY BRANCH

JUJU JAZZ POETICS

By J. Plunky Branch

ISBN 978-1-7379910-0-7

Published by N.A.M.E Brand Records, Richmond, VA

December 4, 2021

Design Concept by Pun Anderson
Art Direction by The Mamou Group

CONTENTS

Haikus

#1

experience shared
makes us smile and suddenly
it's been years and more

#2

a solid shadow
guards the window of my soul
an African mask

#3

morning comes faster
when you are rushing headlong
into the east wind

Juju Is

Juju is African magic, conjured spirits black spells cast
Juju is Congolese outfits scary sculptures and masks
It's Cuban Santeria and Haitian voodoo
It's Jamaican Obeah and Mississippi hoodoo
That's Juju / an induced trance and
Ade Obe or Dele* music at a Lagos dance
A ritual that subverts a debasing word from France
Let them say Juju is a toy, a play thing made
Out of the dialect of a Black prayer prayed
Juju is knowing about irony and euphemisms
(and using) the secret power of African rhythms
In response to enslavement and colonialization
Juju with it's mystification
Has the power to change the collective imagination

*King Sunny Ade, Chief Commander Ebanizer Obe or Dele Abiodun - what else
need we say

A Revolutionary

The low man on the totem pole is the strongest
The victor is the one who lasts the longest
As soon as he becomes a visionary
The slave is a revolutionary

His back is strengthened by his toil
His sweat and blood enrich the soil
His story will be legendary
Once the slave is a revolutionary

Teach the children to take responsibility
Let them learn from our history
Never mind the stories to the contrary
The slave was often a revolutionary

No man knows the hour or exactly when
But the truth crushed to the earth shall rise again
His conditions are always temporary
If the slave becomes a revolutionary

Possession is a motivation
That has hung up an entire nation
Only owners should find it scary
To see the slave as a revolutionary

Righteousness must take a stand
For the victory of every man

About the future there is no worry
Once the slave is a revolutionary

Teach the children to love one another
Cause they're all really sisters and brothers
Hatred of the oppressor is unnecessary
To make the slave a revolutionary

Tyranny tries to crush the feelings
That make liberty all the more appealing
Oppression makes an insurrectionary
Love makes a revolutionary

Jazz Is...

jazz is a state of mind triggered by the sounds of freedom
swinging between this note and the next heart beat
the ahh-h and the aha! of musical surprises
and the happiness associated with angel smiles and dancing feet

jazz is the defiance of souls that only say 'yes'
no matter what the question or the request
fleet fingers running over keys and strings
somber drones and mantras recited to hypnotize the hip
the hip know ties that bind them are forever and temporary
the hip know all the grooves and the standard riffs
they know the titles the subplots and value of the gifts

jazz is the razzmatazz of African spirits meeting at the crossroads
elevating the blues to the status of hymns
being sung to the high heavens even in low dives

Jazz is just music
like the sound of gabriel's horn is just an ordinary fanfare
and thunder is just rolling timpani drums
and lightning is just a light show for the stars and rain
to say that it is only anything is like saying that an emotion is
only love
as if that explains what it is not when that means everything
or so many things
like D-Knowledge says:
and so many more things after those things and more things
after those things

because like so many things jazz is entropic
which means there is always newness and more
and that there is nothing you can do with jazz in jazz or to jazz
that doesn't add to it's complex simplicity
making it more jazz

jazz is a language, a lingo a vernacular of sounds and kinetic
motion

a brewing teapot
and a steamy cauldron of chunky gumbo
to be served by the ladle-full onto old platters and new shining discs
and sucked up by hungry ears

jazz functions somewhere between the inside and the out
moving swiftly and effortlessly from here to there
and back to where   you have never been before
without ever leaving in the first place

jazz is to be continued ...

Jazz Is More

jazz is more
than laying on the floor
drifting over the familiar territory of my room
with John Coltrane taking me back to my future

jazz is a familiar place made new
by the changes in stillness
or by the sameness of anytime
transfigured by a flurry of sonic activity
jazz is being blown away by a whisper
or being absorbed into an explosion
of enlightenment
it is being surrounded and engulfed
by the space between grace notes

jazz is more than the swinging
low tones rumbling
through the guts of would be angels
walking through ghetto parks
celestial juke joints
and other out of the way spaces
it is wordless poetry
over unchoreographed dances
notated in predetermined improvisational terms
like the movements and sounds
dolphins and gulls make in and over
the waves of the blues in a seascape

jazz is more than its mixed lineage
the mother gives form and feeling
the father spirit and soul
or is it the other way around
we give back echoes
of the universal in our individual solos
amplified and reduced by technology
jazz is a sax and synth and a snare
imitating eternal truths
in a nanosecond
it is circular breathing through a chocolate computer chip
using spectral chromatography to measure
the half life of an inspirational big bang

Thelonious was a monk praying
for a better life for us all
he was a member of an order
of adherents and converts
answering and issuing a call
to greatness
cloistered and channeled
away from the mainstream
to run deep and anything but silently
forming a pool of ideas
which overflowed its banks
in waterfalls spiraling upward
to spray droplets of grooving riffs
that continue to return as
rain (sheets of sound)

snow (softly as in the morning resurrection)
dew (condensation based on humility and coolness)
fog (low hanging clouds in front of mirrors)
all dispersed by the winds of changes
permutations and combinations
derivations and dispensations
on what is hip
jazz is more than
contemporary standard smooth acid
retro bop hard new free classical and urban
more than all that
and less too
jazz is a simple turn of a phrase of the gospel
according to miles as sung by a bird
a yardbird a jailbird a myna bird
or any bird imitating dolphy's flute

jazz is the music
played from scores of black symbols
on lines and spaces on cream-colored pages
turned brown and frayed around the edges
with ageless originality

jazz is to be continued...

Breathe

50 Horns Concert

Breathe / We say breathe / Simply breathe
Breathe in in unison / Breathe out in harmony
Just breathe / Breathe in Justice
Breathe out embellishments to the environment
Breathe without prejudgment
In /out / Life calls us to breathe
We respond / Inhaling / Taking life in
Exhaling / Pushing our spirit out / Through this tube
This brass pipe / This tunnel to eternity

When he said "I can't breathe"
He meant he couldn't live / Like this
We shouldn't have to live like this
Under the gun / Under the boot / Under the sun
Under the poverty line
We know the human frailties
Of having the power and the authority
Weaponry and ignorance / Fear and lack of empathy
We know what breeds a vicious disregard for history

We sound the alarm / Of the pounding heart
We sound the trumpet / The call to action
We imitate Gabriel's call to prayer
We breathe through these pipes / Of wood and metal
To echo what we have heard / To blow what we know
To inspire the dance and the word
To imitate and re-create life

We are the army of peace / We wield the power to heal
We are the force / We are the progeny of the ancestors
We are the ones who know / The way the truth and the light
So we blow to show what's right
We breathe / Breathe in / Taking in energy
But more importantly / We breathe out / Giving back more
And with our last breath / We say to the old and the young
Blow your horn / Sing dance carve recite
Seize the day / Challenge the night

Breathe

Our Daughters

our daughters strive to carve out a place
for their natural desires, powers and love
they are so fine and so precious and proud so fragile and strong
they are not waiting for a fairy godmother or glass slipper or a hero
formerly known as a prince
they are the great granddaughters of mother Africa
big boned, lipped and bootied
mysterious voodoo children with innocent smiles
they are coy and seductive
each with a perfect face with lips crinkled
with the lines of agelessness and sex appeal
each with arched eyebrows over eyes like the tigress
nose opened with the scent of her man
this sister forever young
bent at the waist to shake tail feathers and strike a pose
she is always in vogue
her head tilted just so you know that she knows
how much sway she has over you
and whoever will look into those eyes and listen to that voice
and hold on to that waist and feel the wiggle of those hips
there is no hope for them
there is nothing but hope in her heart

she is an actress and a songstress
and a negress and a queen of the nile and the neighborhood
she is the heroine of our story
she's got attitude to match her wardrobe
and heart to match her bold nakedness
her shoulders are strong enough
to bare her share of the responsibility for her culture
and they are broad enough to pull her weight
alongside her man and their children
conscious daughters, sisters of the ebony reality
new moon women, golden ladies, dream lovers,
dream purveyors, dream painters, seducers,
ferocious felines, angels,
just be you

airwalk

Young Brothers

Young brothers' faces reflect
the shades of the black rainbow
lights and shadows ebonys and creams tans and blue hues
A cast of movie of characters from around the way
some with loud voices and nothing to say
others silent with heavy messages behind their eyes
some sing out praises much to our surprise
All of them dressed in the trappings of their peer pressures
These young brothers are the signs of wonderful possibilities
endless rebirths and bright aspirations unabashed fertility
they are owners of the next wave
entrepreneurs of dreams and managers of the music of the spheres
and when we really listen their hip-hop dreams bring smiles to our ears
They are our man children
innocent of the sins of their forefathers
and to be forgiven for their own
they should be free of the fat of overindulgence
yet they are in danger of falling
into the death of complacency and unwarranted contentment
which is so different from letting it be and going with the flow
if it's up to us to tell them they should already know
beauty is in the eyes of the beheld

beauty is in the joy of life
and these our offspring are the beautiful
they are full of energy, full of the light
which sparks between the atoms of their being
they give us hope and reasons to keep the faith
no matter what we're seeing
so we must do all in our power
to aid them in their quest for phat futures
dope destinies and rapid reparations
the revolution is now about lasting legacies
and leaving something for our sons and their grandchildren

Juju Can You Feel It

This is juju /can u feel it / it's persuasive / like African odor
it's pervasive if you perceive it and if you receive its subtle
aroma, and realize, like you can find treasure in a yard full of
junk / there are seductive pheromones in the funk

Like the after taste of a wine bouquet affects the smell of the
words you say
Or like enjoying the afterglow before you go away
Your mind is opened to the possibilities because of your sensibilities
Your awareness is the result of rituals
offerings that were sacrificial

Yes you paid the price of admission / to be in the privileged condition
of getting up after falling / and submerging your will to that
of a higher calling
The vocation of the griot / whose job it is to know
The speaker and the hearer / the healed and healer
The father and the son
The teacher and the learner, all as one, all is one, oneness, the
oneness of juju, can you feel it…

Sometimes

Sometimes is it important to test our senses by touching
something and maybe getting burned

Every once in a while testing our intuition by going against it
and maybe getting hurt, is how we learn

That's one way to verify what we otherwise would only have
thought we knew better

Learning from experience is how to learn to interpret the
nuances of new, the subtleties of substances unseen

Sometimes the times we don't listen to our inner voice are as
important as the times that we do

Sometimes the glass is half empty and sometimes the glass is
half full

If you got a glass with something in it then it's all good
It's all good

Sometimes some time is all good
It's all good all the time

Blackness

I am this / I am that / You can't miss that I am black
Everybody likes something, that's a fact
Everybody likes something, something black

Black music black culture black people black minds
Black arts black magic black history black times
Black power black skills black skin black & proud
Black African Black leaders black voices say it loud

Black holes Black words black thought black world
Black man black woman black boy black girl
Black Panther black cat black ball black unity
Black studies Black pride in the Black community

Black Jesus Black Madonna black angels black sea
Black gold black water black ice black like me
Black sky black cloud black star black night
Black Mariah black Jew black & blue black & white

Black berry Black English black Russian black beast
Black smoke Black Fire black war black peace
Black theater black comedy Black Sambo in black face
Black dance black jazz black heritage black race

Black label black mamba Black board jungle big black snake
Black bird black bitch little black book black is great
Black church black caucus black folks on the black hand side
Black slaves black workers black graves of blacks who died

Black pearl black rock black olive Black roots
Black dog Black ghetto black shoes black boots
Black & nappy black top black wisdom black knowledge
Black problem black revolution black solution black college

Black coffee black ink Black Nationalist integration
Black mail black widow of black exploitation
Black witch in the black Black Strap molasses
Black head black tie affairs for Black middle classes

Black African Negro Afro American Black
Black black you can't take it back
Black is black If you're Black — get back

The creator has a master plan
It's a black thing I hope you understand

Fade to black

Living My Life As A Jazz Solo

1. I Am Streams and Screams and recurring themes / I riff
by cutting and pasting strands of intertwined melodies that
spiral like ribbons of DNA / combined in a unique way
to be me and my songs. I am inherited recurring themes
reminders of where we've been and where we're going and
by all means / Making time, or taking mine out of the quiet
spots / surrounded by the hotspots / while being so cool.
My diatonic scales come in waves of be-bop and the waves
never stop. They could become a drone of the ordinary, but
like Bird / my every ebbing tide is potentially the last word
depending on how and when I'm heard.

2. Living my life as a jazz solo, I learned to fly. I learned to fly
by riding a pendulum between two rhythms like on a trapeze
swinging with ease / between the pre- known and the now I
see / swinging over beats like 1, 2, 3 / pushed, no pulled back
to the future and ahead to the past / between tradition and
newness, from the roots up through the grass / to the highs
and sighs of the leaves on trees blowing in the breeze.

3. I am recurring themes / and melodies created out of impulses and dreams / and reflections / like when I look through the window out on to the sea, and see, at the same time, the reflection of the scene behind me / in the room and, at the same time, be aware of the glass itself and at the same time, see myself with three eyes. This is a set of viewpoints that expose a set of new points, new perspectives that cannot be re-covered, that unlike a jack-in-the-box cannot be put back in the box, that cannot be un-seen and forgotten because, having once been a genie and knowing one's potential, it is impossible to not be.

4. Like a jazz solo I am different grooves at different tempos harmonized / restructured and inverted like you never heard it / smoothly hip / when I downshift into a mellow dip / non-rushed and un-paused / firmly rooted in the cause educated in the rules/ schooled in being cool / and self-taught in views found in the baptismal pool / full-bodied, deep toned and getting deeper still / self-confident with a super strong will / I be styling and profiling / quoting great lines and stimulating great minds / on a roll and blowing down I be throwing / while spiraling ever upwards till I'm free / Free / as Ornette/ Free / as bird / Free / as the wind Free / as fire / Free/ as I dream / as I stream! As I beam! AS I Scream! AS I Scream! AS I Scream! My recurring themes...

Living my life as a jazz solo…

Black Fire
for Jimmy Gray

a black fire burns at your core
spreading a warmth that radiates
through your love of our music
expressing itself through your words and deeds
low key and in the background
yet boisterous and smoothed with lots of reverb
your strength is in your voiced opinions
and in your ability to improvise on a theme
take an idea and run with it in your mouth
stop on a sixteenth note and spit it out
as a riff in a solo
or a whimsical rhyming couplet
followed by a chuckle
to relieve the listener of the need to be serious
but you are always serious
serious i say
seer-ious as a soothsayer
a forward reacher just slightly ahead of this time
panasonic and panchromatic
like melodious chaos and multiple shades of ebony
you have vision
tunneled and expansive
you are a producer and a transducer
a resister and a transistor
a performer and a transformer

a defender and a transcender
a realist and a surrealist
blending colors to refracture images of the light in your eyes
your graying afro forms a halo to hold your apple jack cap
your chewstick is a symbol of quiet charisma
reminding you and others of your connection
to other times and unlimited dimensions
your fastings and your musical diet have made you wizened
beyond those ten years you are my senior
i'd like to think i'm smarter
but time and then again some little film clip of a digital
sample of a snippet of something that you said to me after i
said it to you in the first place comes back around to haunt
me for not saying that yeah you predicted that it would come
to pass and that your name for it would be the nommo that
would cast just the right spell to blend the juju and the blues
to make the funk jazz juice that would serve as a medicinal
balm for the computer induced viral complacency of a new age
i should have said it before
well i'm saying it now in this poem
your ideas spark and enkindle with improvised whimsy
you are an inspiration
keep on burning
black fire!

For Ornette

You blew lines and angles / made tracks from Fort Worth to
LA / took the A train from 59th down to SoHo and created
your own stop on Prince Street / your vamps cut short and
elongated overarching simple but universal themes / stars and
stripes in skies over America / timelessness / mindfulness.
Happiness / nappiness / topless / spotless / formless
loneliness in homelessness hominess your home everywhere-
ness meant keyless entries past purist sentries.

You used your sax as a tool, a toy, a telescope, a stethoscope,
your sax as a plastic probe, a weapon of peace around the
globe, you were a questioner, a why-not suggestioner, a
one note at a time harmonizer, a blue note demonizer, a
compassionate naïve synthesizer

Your sax was like a drum, a violin / a brass, a wood wind
A metal cone with ivory keys / with your life's breath blown
across vibrating reeds

Some reach for evermore complexity but you knew ultimate
intricacy was achieved by utter simplicity
You knew the intimacy of one love one peace one music and
you used it to serenade a lonely woman

In prime time / you wore rainbows and tuxedos / with attitude
that said satin suits me / with a style that said choose me or
lose me / all a while wearing a cherubic half smile
punctuated and articulated with a tongue lisp and accentuated
with a saxy tongue kiss

You stitched together patches of blues in many hues
seamlessly generating news and newness
Endlessly until you finished inside out and free

Maintaining Rhythms
for Janine

Rhythms in time; rhythms in your mind. Rhythm streams.
Rhythms from deep in the Nile and the Zambezi / rhythms
that quicken your heart and give you hope / even as your
pains want to rush up through your throat / as screams
against despair / the rhythms take you pass even there.

Your urge to create a new life for yourself is your birthright
and a gift from God. Powers that be within you always, again
make themselves known. Inner strength comes from having
a vision of how things will be if you can maintain; maintain
a daily commitment to maintaining. Maintain / a discipline
over what you will take into your body and brain / and in
time / new vistas will be painted on the canvas of your mind.
Maintain. Maintain with the aid of fellow travelers who have
been down Tobacco roads through Old Havana outback to
Kumasi and back over to Cabrini, South Central, South East
and Church Hill. Maintain with mentors and sponsors who
have re-collections of their own reflections from the pieces
of shattered mirrors in their big mama's house. Saints who
fall down and then get up and then say to us, "Maintain!"

Maintain. Maintain the rhythm. Maintain the gain. Maintain the flow by being as ready to give, as you are ready to think that you ought to be receiving. Maintain the main frame: your mind, your body, your dome / your spirit, your vibes and your home / Maintain, don't let your energy wane, not when you've come this far, journeyed so far to get here, to right now, when you have this momentous moment, this dynamite day, this pulsating pause, this validating, culminating, unmitigating minute that you've been waiting for, waiting and waiting some more for, went through the open door for, and then waited some more for.

Maybe you shouldn't be waiting no more. Maybe you should be doing even more, moving more, working and searching for more, burning and yearning for more and earning more time, to find / the rhythms from deep in the Congo River that is your blood.

So Amazing
for Jackie after her concert

They poured out accolades like libations to a goddess
lavished praises on you as if it was your world
and you ruled it with wisdom and grace
After you sang your perpetual uplifting carol
using that voice that resonates with richness and purity
causing nearby heart strings and other things to vibrate and tingle
they clapped and lifted up hosannas
They honored your strength and serenity
your dedication and piety
your poise and generosity
wishing you continued success
hoping that you would stay among them
wishing for great things for you
hoping you would continue share a reflection of their best
Friends and family coworkers and bosses
spoke of outward bonds and business things
while silently vibing on being blessed by your presence
They gushed critical acclaim for your music
displayed expanding esteem for your outstanding work
and marveled that your tone resounds even deeper with time

Many tried to express something
to show appreciation for your golden airs
a word a smile a gift a prayer an amen a compliment a shiver a tear
anything worthy of your capacity to embody so much love
A chorus of so many sang such high praises to your talents
but most astounding is that you deserved it all
earned all that glowing respect
through long days humming hymns while sowing seeds
through short nights singing while sewing pearls on your white
gown of glory
You are a humble high priestess of soulful songs
a siren and lover and spiritual mother of many sons and daughters
You are so amazing

She was always...
for Lorna

she was always /so vibrant, so robust, thick with joy
so positive, encouraging and positive again after that
she was always / so uplifting and complimentary
because she was always looking for the good
and giving the benefit of the doubt
she was always / so energetic
and bold of spirit / big hearted, big boned, big bottomed
big and black, and giving big ups to our blackness
black like me, black like the night with stars in her eyes
and black like the stars in her crew
she was always / not fragile or feeble in any way
nothing about her said weakness or delicate or breakable
she was always / brave and daring and always caring
she took on risks as if she knew the outcomes
would be worthy of her energy
worthy of her soulful journey
she was always / working while singing, chanting, spitting verses
recognizing and cultivating the talents around her
and it was always around her
drawn to the brightness beaming from her smile and her being
she was always / so much more than what met the eye
so much more about giving than getting

so much more than words and verses
she was always / doing her thing
which was teaching us how to live and give unabashedly
how to be effusive with our applause, our praise
our encouragement of each other
she was always / sharing wisdom beyond her years
and always so young at heart
I am sure she wouldn't want us to shed tears
instead she'd want us to remember how
she was always / there for us
she was always / going and going
she was always / on her way, up higher, soaring
on her way home and now she has arrived
and we must and will survive
now she is always / there to remind us that:
life is a brutally honest loving cycle
life is short sweet fragile and happy when we're smiling
like she was / always …

My Daughter
for Kaila

My daughter is so badass!
High maintenance high energy hi octane & highly efficient
She is beyond terrific
Terrifying to anything / anyone
Less than... aspirational

She ignores boundary-setters!
Oh she sees them
but bounds over around and thru those
trying to limit her possibilities
change her destination
Or do not understand hers is the way

She is principal of her home school!
Chief operations officer of a media conglomerate
And cutie-pie sexy mama
Ignoring heads she turns
As she strides purposefully and expediently
On to her next appointment

She is a phenomenal woman of so many superlatives
So much energy and dynamism
I am so proud of the example she sets for her offspring
I nearly burst at the realization
She is mine

Yoga for Retirement
for Dawn

Breathe in / stretch out / do everything / you care about
then wait / you won't be late / to get to where / you should
be / When you go from here / you'll be there

Be flexible / and stretchable / to bend / go with the Zen
to get in / the position / you envision / Then take time
to clear your mind / it's a blessing / to just be / anywhere
when you see / there / are lessons / of life / everywhere

Be teachable / and reachable / only struggle / when you
decide / it's worth the trouble / of plans and schemes
No effort / is wasted / once you've tasted / the sweetness
of reachable dreams

Take steps / one at a time / but after six / or seven
find heaven / in the resting / to recharge / your best thing is
the pause / for the cause / because / if all things
are considered / it's in the quiet ordinary moments
when wonders are delivered

So even as you retire / and no longer hire / and fire / it
doesn't take a sage / to know / that even at this age / when
all is said / and done / the best / is yet to come

Teeth in a Jar

Getting new false teeth is crossing an invisaline
Crossing an invisible but undeniable bridge into older age.
More senior than simple AARP eligibility. For real though.
Soul for real, so old for real. So for real
Teeth in a jar by the sink
Missing from the masticating routine
Missing from the smile on both sides of the mirror
Is a sculpture of an unmasked robber of optimism
Like a bad weather forecast
Or the thought that you might never have new love
So you'd better take great care of the ones you have now
It is a revelation

Does it all go downhill from here
Down into a gaping space
Into the abyss of a false negative narrative
No because memories are mostly marvelous
A rewriting of history
A re-creation of a story about fantasy and promise
Like the picture of my new smile
Whole and handsome from any angle

False teeth is a misnomer
Because the new smile is so for real
Like the new optimism it speaks to
Okay so maybe there are more seasons
And more reasons to keeping loving living smiling and giving

Will you still love me tomorrow
When I take them out
And am without the handsome self-image
Not acting the self-confident Romeo
Are gum jobs real and will you want one
Will you close your eyes and only see the new guy
15 years ago
Nibbling at your coochie
Will you be able to get past the image of your grandfather
Trying to get you hot / maybe not

The reality of false teeth causes the realization of the
inevitability of real finality
That everything is truly all right
Pain loss endings beginnings meltings helpings mads glads all alright
Memories orgasms birthday cakes friends babies all alright
Coltrane's favorite things warm breezes and comings and goings
More than all right
And then
Best of all
You knew me when

I Know

As an abstract idea, I am not sure I need somebody to love.
But I know that I want you concretely, completely, discreetly,
so sweetly and so deeply. I love you.

As a theory, I don't know if I need anybody else. But I know I
need you seriously, mysteriously, deliriously, imperiously I love
you.

As a meditation, I know love is everywhere, but in practice it is
where you are mostly, or when you approach me, closely (even
if ghostly), I love you.

As a general rule, I am very independent, but I know I need
you, heed you, I bleed you, indeed you made me need you. I
love you.

Hypothetically I'm in complete control of my emotions, but
theoretically, empathetically, steadily and readily I have fallen
for you.

As a presumption. I am innocent and without desires, But I
know you light my fire, you're all I require, you inspire me, I
love you.

Fidelity

fidelity is beyond the physical

there is nothing casual about love's intimacy

it is intense and intended

craved and yearned for

wanted and desired

and just happens

...it just happens

Lake Michigan Muse

I journeyed half way round the world
to a longed-for inland sea
and it was like a coming home
for the waves had called to me

I had seen the undulating swells
in my dreams
but it was always at night
and the shoreline wore the skyline
like a bejeweled necklace

When you came out day broke
and your face was in the foreground
of an expansive seascape
and your body's outline gave shape
to the possibilities of sensuality
Your scent caused the shimmering
of the sunlight on the waves
green now in your aura
wafting rhythmically
imitating your dance

Poetry and jazz are feelings
glimpses of spirituality and humor

The dance is a moving picture
A short movie about sensations
Your kuumba and your karma
are all these things and many others
and their effects on me
are mental and visual
physical and touch sensitive
reflective and internalized
mysterioso like a Monk
solo live in Paris
or juju in Nigeria
polyrhythmic in its repercussions

I sit at your feet
gently touching the hem of your sheer garment
you glance at me and time stops
as if frozen in the folds of one of the cowerie shells
in your bracelet
With a snap of your fingers
the celestial clocks spring forward
leaving me dizzy and falling
deeper in love

You dance when you walk
parts of you jiggle in time
with the beat of your steps

Your eyes and your moves hypnotize
and remind me that I am compelled
to want you

Is there nobility in denial
Can there be spiritually in fasting

I came halfway round the world
to a great inland sea
I enjoyed the waters
though I did not drink or swim
The waters receded from the earth
leaving flat plains and mountains
I came to see that the waters do dance
and you went with me to the edge of flight
to leave me smiling and in waiting
Until the next time....

Summer Shower Solitude

When it finally rained I was at home alone
and soon I was thinking
how much I wanted you with me
right then and now
The music of the downpour
the grayness of the sheets of sound
put me in the mood

I roamed all over the house thinking of you
Out on the front porch
I watched the raindrops dance on the pavement
and remembered
how my mother used to pretend
the splashes were people
singing "Run, people, run!"

I walked into the living room
past the African statues silently standing guard
over the plants and my idealism
I closed a window to keep out the spray
and smiled at the muffled sound of the downpour
and how the looks on the female masks
made me think of our kinship –
tribal and romantic

In solitude I walked through the house
searching for the perfect setting
and accompaniment for my feelings
I turned off the light in the dining room

and the computer in the office den
grabbed a beer in the kitchen
checked the windows everywhere
even in the bathroom
where it is not unusual to be alone
with water and thoughts
I decided not to float on the bed
in the chamber where I sleep
I picked up binoculars
and used them to fly
over the backyards and garage tops
in the neighborhood
imagining that the gray veil of rain was a curtain
at the window of a London flat
and the sheds and alleys and backs of houses
were in the perpetual fog of that city
as I was then and last spring

The downpour drenched me
in a thick dark sentimental mood
The sound of the water falling
was the drone of a weather motor
propelling me upward
Lightning now and again preceded thunder claps
then there was just the rain
soaking everything everywhere
with life giving fluid and a new age music

I settled on the front porch
alone in the world
witnessing the flow of the wetness everywhere
alone with my shivers and thoughts of you
and too much rain for the gutters and down spouts

Far off in the distance there were subtle timpani rolls
anchoring and punctuating
the rises and falls of the glissandos from the eaves
Focusing on the mid range
the drone of masses of drops became the background
for the tinkling splashes of those hitting in proximity
to my disposition and my thoughts
which are closer to me than my breath

My awareness extends beyond this body
seated under the protection of my verandah
My influence reaches past the boundary of this house
and the property line
My emotions are affected by emanations
from inside the beats of my heart
and by phenomena from as far away
as the starting point of the rains
which have come after such a long dry spell
to put me in this mood

Eventually the cloud burst symphony ends
A new etude begins
trickles, drips, droplets
compose after the rain refrains
A breeze blowing is one of my favorite things
I am gratified
A drought has ended
I have spent this time
alone and with you
I am comfortable and satisfied with those two
Together

Poem #10

the white egret stood tall on its spindly legs at the black
waters edge at two a.m.

it was a sight to behold with its curved neck and majestic
though small stature

was it real or an apparition meant to freeze my thoughts
in time and make me wonder about things beautiful yet
seemingly out of place

the waves of the lake shimmered and glistened in the
shadows without the benefit of moon or star lights

does anyone else know that you are out here at this time of
night alone at the lake or am i simply the last one to know
about your presence

the egret was not really out of place but in an inner city park
not in a reserve or in the wild but in its native state of virginia

i was struck by the sight of this stately egret as i drove by and this caused me to slow down my car which caused the bird to spread its wings and move just a bit in preparation for flight if needed

the white bird against the black waters of the lake with gray middle of the night sky overhead was right out of a dream or off my album cover in the picture that denny painted which was also printed onto the bright shiny compact disc itself

the white egret so graceful and beautiful was you or your vibe sent to me like an image scanned from your spirit and beamed into my night to put me in a dream-state to remind me of all the things you are and all the possibilities that are here and now realized

i've got to go back to the lake tomorrow which is actually later today to see if the egret or the dream is still there

to whom it may concern

in these silent moments
I am comforted by my thoughts of you
and by remembrances of things gone by
yet still here with me

I am numbed by new lessons
relearned again and again
and now I know that there is little to be gained
by caution
and nothing to be gained from fear
of loss and pain

enough love is certainly its own reward
shared feelings are so valuable
that potential embarrassment is nothing
in comparison
I should be embarrassed
to have ever harbored such fears
but I am not

I now know that I must share my joys
with those on whom I depend for them
I will pass on a kind word
encouragement and laurels
to all who pass my way

it's the least that I should do
for those who give me so much happiness
and so many insights
and to you
especially to you

please know that I love you
and that I have depended on your energy
and the experiences you bring
the questions you raise
the reactions you instigate
and the emotions and dreams you inspire

please forgive me that this message
has been so long coming
almost lost in the pile of undeliverable mail
unwritten or never faxed to your number
but not too late
to be reflected back in these feelings
I have when I am alone
and thinking of you
hearing the echoes of your smile
and feeling your closeness

The Revolution / Don't Miss It This Time

"The revolution will not be televised."
Gil Scott-Heron

"Niggas are scared of revolution."
The Last Poets

"The revolution is not coming, the revolution is now."
Juju, A Message From Mozambique

The revolution is being televised, video taped and marketed as we speak
A revolution is happening on computer monitors all over the
world wide web
A revolution was shown in a documentary about the Chinese
student-led, pro-democracy movement and massacre at Tiananmen
Square on Cinemax, on Cinemax! and it was dope, slammin'
politically correct, moving, instructive, inspiring, it named names,
showed the faces of people in the struggle for liberation, was a
victory for the people, it showed the suffering of the people, and
their tears and their sweat and their spilled blood and their dashed
hopes, and it was uplifting and optimistic and it was real and it was
on Netflix
The revolution will happen in the minds of the people
The revolution happens universally, globally, internationally and in
single cells
A revolution will happen on cablevision
The revolution can only be confirmed in terms of mass
consciousness raised
A revolution will happen when we have a million family march
A revolution is happening as you take this all in
The revolution will happen behind closed eye lids
A revolution will happen in Burundi and Nigeria and Brazil and
Guatemala and…
The revolution will happen when we know what we gonna do after that
The revolution will be happening when we are as dedicated as

the Reverend William Barber and when we put in as many hours
as Korean shopkeepers and when we are as supportive of our
extended families are they are and when we work as hard as
sweatshop seamstresses and migrant farm labor organizers for
ourselves and when we work as hard as Zulu miners with each
other and when we are willing to think as much as the planners
before the demonstrations and when we are willing to work as
much as those who clean up after them
The revolution will be happening when we work as hard as the
leaders we criticize when we give as much as honest lawyers and
when we sacrifice as much as poor righteous preachers
The revolution will happen when we work harder than those
working against it
A revolution is not happening unless it is shown on youtube & CNN
The revolution will happen in a state of mind
A revolution is happening on various sized screens all over the world
The world is being Americanized and this is an ongoing revolution
driven by music, movies, magazine ads, videos, infomercials and
technology in general
The Black revolution of the sixties would not be televised because
niggars were scared of revolution despite the activities of the
Panthers, US, Move, Cultural nationalists, rheteritionists, poets and
socialists but back then they didn't have computers, e-mail, facetime
or virtual reality, now we're ready / now what's your excuse
The African-American revolution will happen when we visualize
what we would do after said revolution and move on it now, when
we see our future and be about it now, when we learn from our
past and live out the lessons now / when we amalgamate the
wisdom of our ancestors with the technology of now / when we
take back the hoods from the hoods and transform them into our
own, when we are able to produce our own televised reality now.
The next revolution will happen when the concept of the 13th
monkey is actualized and a critical mass of us are awakened to new
thought consciousness and raise the energy level of the planet to a
higher vibration

The revolution is being digitized and entered into the virtual reality of your brain, but can you dig it and are you preparing your kids for it, to be in it / to reap the return on your investment; or are you invested in it or down with it at all? The revolution will be televised, but as a rerun and a mini-series that you missed the first time around because you were scared to watch for fear that you might be seen and asked to do something or you might have been connected to the conspiracy and lose your job The revolution of the spirit is all it takes to be changed in the twinkling of an eye   forever

Free your mind and everything else will follow
The revolution is not coming
So you won't miss it next time
Free your mind
Don't miss it this time

who didn't know

who didn't know
that most of the drugs in hood don't grow in the hood
but come by planes boats trains and big trucks
and none of the dealers on the block own planes
most have never even been on a boat
and the few who have taken the amtrak went on a school class trip
or with their moms to visit some relative
most of the hood-dweller-dealers are the mom and pop variety
who don't even realize that to supply herb for all the smokers
for just one city for just one week
you need it by the tractor trailer load

who didn't know that
some of the ones who make big time quantities of big time money
from drugs are bankers CIA operatives and ex-military officers
who have access to planes and boat and trains
and who know the communication schemes and the porousness
of the interdiction smoke screens
who have buddies and ex-subordinates still in the service and
the agencies
who will aide and abet or look the other way
or simply won't just say no
and the beats and the games and the big business grows on

who didn't know that
crack cocaine is a most insidious drug that goes right to the
pleasure center in the brain
artificially taking away the pain
while depleting the brain of key chemicals needed to naturally
feel good again

meaning the user becomes the usee
inevitably eventually becoming dependent on the potent
numbing agent
for any kind of enjoyment from love to employment
leaving them to wonder where the hour went
up in smoke like their self-empowerment

who didn't know that
alcohol is a drug
and so is nicotine and caffeine
just ask the coffee drinking cigarette smoking dope fiend
at the bar after work it's miller time and weekends were made
for michelob
but these dopes have been made respectable and legal
by the same people that want to keep herb illegal

who didn't know that
jails are full of young bloods who took a bum chance
on a dumb dance with the devil

... if you made drugs legal
who would have the most to lose
our communities or the prison builders
glaucoma and cancer patients
or the CIA, laundering banks in switzerland and miami,
argentina and peruvian military
drug lords with connections in france
... it doesn't take the whole army to be smugglers
or all of the agents to be covert big time pushers
or all the cops to be on the take
to pollute the system and corrupt the whole process
just a few will do
but who didn't know that

Questions

Why should gangsta rappers be our spokespersons
Why should they be the black guys we see and hear the most
on tv cable and radio
Why not listen to the young men who teach and oversee the
little ones on the playground of the day care center
or the ones that work at the drug store check-out counter
by day and go to school at night

Is it that it is more interesting to hear about gang banging than
personal development
Is it more useful to hear about tech nines than computer tech
and more sensible to talk about being blunted than being clear
headed enough to ask the right questions

Is it that the boys stuck in the hood trapped by the insensitivity
of the larger society and indifferent to the pain they cause
themselves and the suffering they cause their families make
more interesting stories than those inner-city young people
who converse and debate and struggle to get something done
other than just getting over

Is it that we all are titillated by danger; and the danger of
hoods in the hood to each other is more alluring than the
danger they pose to those who would like to change the hoods
into something better

Is it that we are attracted to fear and loathing and we fear the
rappers with their pants hanging off their asses more than we
fear what will happen if they influence the righteous young
men and women to fail

Is it that the low down and dirty mouth lyricists can speak
for us in more graphic and exciting terms than young poets
who have listened to baraka, madhabukti, jessie jackson,
muhammad ali, ossie davis, the last poets and the best of the
bold black voices

Do we let corporate "others" promote thug life because they
don't speak to us, "it's just a young folks' thing and they'll grow
out of it" / or is it that we don't see that so many young folks
are dying before they get old enough to grow out of it

Are the young dealers of inexperienced rancor and untutored
street lore allowed to speak for our community because we
trust them more than ones we send to get a higher education

Do the nasty and the uncouth get the phat beats and the phat
contracts because they are more creative and are more saleable
or isn't it time to check out the rhythms that young black
conscious artists are drumming out and then hype that funk

Or are we making those decisions / Who is then and what are
you to them

Who speaks for Israel, the Palestinians, the Canadians, who
are the voices in South Africa, China, England, not just
governmentally but artistically? why then should rhyming
fools from south central or cabreeni or bedstuy speak for us, if
what they're representin' is only negative repercussions and not
positive alternatives

Are these guys speaking for us because we have lost our voices
or do we think that who's talking isn't the issue and what
they're saying don't mean a thing cause it ain't swinging

Have we totally forgotten the power of the word, nommo
Then it's time to remember ancestral lessons and that the
voices of the people
reflect their spirit and affect their spirit;

Only those who can inspire us should be given a platform and a mic
MCs should be masters of something more than meaningless
or vengeful rhymes
freestyle should be about style and freedom

It's time to know what time it is and if you don't know
you better ask not just any somebody but somebody who's
studying themselves and their history and international trends
and movements and if they don't know the answers they got
enough sense to know where to go look and how to get 411
on the internet or on the vibe line connecting us all to the
universal creator

Or have we been numbed to yelling and the screaming and the
ravings and the dealing by the sheer volume and the massive
doses of the bull shit and now we just don't give a damn

love makes us better

Every word implies its counterpart / like finishing and start
Like opposite and attract / like heart and attack
Music like love makes us better / better and better
Better than ever
This is important to keep in mind
As we navigate life and time
Dropping knowledge is like raising Kane / lifting spirits
Again and again
Raising Gyland the Blue Gorilla is as vital as lifting J Dilla
That's beside the point of reference and reverence
This point is relevant
To what came before, to what opened the doors
To higher consciousness
Going by way of good then better
To be our best
And sharing love, giving love, seeing love everywhere
Being love and showing we care
Always and forever
Love makes us better
Better and better

Saxophonist J. Plunky Branch is an accomplished performer, songwriter, producer and musicologist. Plunky co-founded Black Fire Records and heads N.A.M.E. Brand Records — through which he has released 30 albums and composed over 450 songs.

His autobiography, *Plunky: Juju Jazz Funk & Oneness – A Musical Memoir,* was published in 2015. He has produced three documentary films, including *Under the Radar: A Survey of Afro-Cuban Music,* shot in Cuba in 2001.

In 2018, J. Plunky Branch received the prestigious "50 For 50 Award" from the Virginia Commission for the Arts as one of the 50 outstanding arts persons in Virginia of the last 50 years. In 2015 he was selected as one of the "Strong Men & Women in Virginia History" by the Library of Virginia.

Juju Jazz Poetics is the first volume of poetry from Plunky, with a second volume and two books of song lyrics forthcoming.

Throughout his career, Plunky has entertained and taught thousands, and in the process has developed a broad and loyal following. Well into his seventh decade, he continues to produce new music and films while performing internationally.